# Jackie Joyner-Kersee
## Record-Breaking Runner

Liza N. Burby

The Rosen Publishing Group's
PowerKids Press™
New York

Published in 1997 by The Rosen Publishing Group, Inc.
29 East 21st Street, New York, NY 10010

First Edition

Book Design: Erin McKenna

Photo Credits: Cover and pp. 7, 8, 12, 20 © AP/Wide World Photos, Inc.; p. 4 © 1992 LPI/M. Yada/FPG International Corp.; p. 11 © Frank A. Cezus/FPG International Corp.; pp. 15, 16 © Peter Read Miller 1994/FPG International Corp.; p. 19 © Thomas Zimmermann/FPG International Corp.

Burby, Liza N.
    Jackie Joyner-Kersee / by Liza N. Burby
        p.     cm. — (Making their mark: women in sports)
    Includes index.
    Summary: Covers the life and achievements of the record-breaking runner, Jackie Joyner-Kersee.
    ISBN 0-8239-5064-6 (library bound)
    1. Joyner-Kersee, Jacqueline, 1962– —Juvenile literature. 2. Women track-and-field athletes—United States—Biography—Juvenile Literature. [1. Joyner-Kersee, Jacqueline, 1962– . 2. Track-and-field athletes. 3. Afro-Americans—Biography. 4. Women—Biography.] I. Title. II. Series: Burby, Liza N. Making their mark.
GV697.J69B87 1997
796.42'092—dc21
[B]
                                   96–53335
                                       CIP
                                       AC

Manufactured in the United States of America

# Contents

# Dreaming of a Better Life

Even as a little girl, Jackie Joyner understood that life is not always easy. She was born on March 3, 1962, to teenage parents. Her family had very little money. She grew up in the city of East St. Louis, Illinois. The area where she lived was very **dangerous** (DAYN-jer-us). Jackie wanted to do whatever she could to have a better life when she got older. She was willing to work as hard as she could to make that happen.

◀ Jackie worked hard to make a better life for herself.

# A Young Runner and Jumper

Around the corner from Jackie's home was the Mary E. Brown Community Center. It was a safe place for the **neighborhood** (NAY-ber-hood) children to play. The center was where Jackie first learned that she loved to play sports. She also learned that she was very good at them. Jackie was nine years old when she entered her first **track-and-field** (TRAK-and-FEELD) race. She lost, but she did not give up. By the time Jackie was twelve, she was the best runner and jumper in her neighborhood.

Jackie's positive attitude helped her get ahead in sports. ▶

# Jackie Tries the Pentathlon

Jackie was so good at sports that she didn't do just one. Her coaches at the center asked her to try the **pentathlon** (pen-TATH-lon). A pentathlon has five parts. It includes running, three different kinds of jumps, and throwing a heavy weight, called a shot put, to see how far it can go. Jackie was only fourteen when she won her first pentathlon. She decided then that one day she would win a gold medal at the Olympics.

◀ Jackie combined her running and jumping skills to become a great hurdler.

# The Finest Athlete in Illinois

While she was in high school, Jackie ran track and field, and played basketball and volleyball. A sportswriter named her the finest athlete in the state of Illinois. On the track, she set an Illinois high school **record** (REH-kerd) with her **long jump** (LONG JUMP). She won the junior long jump two years in a row. She did well in her schoolwork too. In 1980, she finished high school with one of the highest grades in her class.

Jackie set her first track-and-field ▶ records in high school.

# Jackie Meets Bob Kersee

Jackie had two **goals** (GOHLS) in mind. She wanted to go to college. She also wanted to **compete** (kum-PEET) at the 1984 Olympics in Los Angeles. She earned a basketball **scholarship** (SKAH-ler-ship) to the University of California at Los Angeles, or UCLA. She hadn't been there long when her mother died. The UCLA track coach, Bob Kersee, became her friend. His mother had died when he was young, too. He saw that Jackie was a very good runner and asked if he could coach her.

◀ Bob saw Jackie's running talent in college and knew he could help her reach her goals.

# Training for the Heptathlon

By 1981, Jackie was still playing basketball, but she was also working on her skills in track and field. Although Jackie's favorite sports event was the long jump, Bob told her that she should train for the **heptathlon** (hep-TATH-lon), which has two more events than the pentathlon. Bob believed that Jackie could be the best heptathlete in the United States.

The javelin is one of the events in the heptathlon. ▶

# Asthma

In 1983, Jackie learned that she had **asthma** (AZ-muh). This sometimes made it hard for her to breathe. The doctor told her not to play sports. But Jackie found a way to control her asthma so she could still train for the Olympics. Jackie worked hard to take care of herself. She took medicine and got a lot of rest. Then, at the 1984 Olympics, Jackie hurt her leg. She lost the gold medal by a few seconds, but Jackie won the silver medal for second place.

◀ Jackie rests between races to control her asthma.

# A Gold Medal at Last

When Jackie graduated from UCLA, she and Bob were married. She started training for the 1988 Olympics. While she was training, she broke her own records. She won the Sullivan Memorial Trophy as one of the world's best **amateur** (AH-mah-cher) athletes. At the 1988 Olympics in Seoul, Korea, Jackie won the gold medal of her dreams in the heptathlon. She also won a gold medal in the long jump with a 24-foot, $3\frac{1}{2}$ inch long jump. This was longer than anyone had ever jumped before.

One of Jackie's favorite ▶ events is the long jump.

# Jackie Makes Sports History

At the 1992 Olympics in Barcelona, Spain, Jackie became the first woman in history to win two heptathlon gold medals in a row. She also won a bronze medal in the long jump. At the 1996 Olympics in Atlanta, Georgia, at the age of 34, Jackie won the bronze medal in the long jump. She had done all she dreamed of doing at the Olympics. She decided to stop competing in the Olympics. Now Jackie has returned to the first sport she ever loved. She is now playing **professional** (pro-FESH-in-ul) basketball.

◀ As a world-class athlete, Jackie has made America proud.

# The Greatest Athlete Ever

Jackie has been called one of the greatest athletes who ever lived. Even with all her success, she has never forgotten where she started. She gives money to cities to build community centers for kids to play sports. She believes that the most important thing for her to do is to tell young people that if they set a goal and work hard, they can make their dreams come true.

# Glossary

**amateur** (AH-mah-cher)  Someone who plays a sport for fun, not to make money.

**asthma** (AZ-muh)  An illness that sometimes makes it hard for someone to breathe.

**compete** (kum-PEET)  To try to win something.

**dangerous** (DAYN-jer-us)  Something that is not safe.

**goal** (GOHL)  Something a person works toward meeting.

**heptathlon** (hep-TATH-lon)  A contest in which athletes have to finish seven different events.

**long jump** (LONG JUMP)  A contest in which the winner is the person who jumps the farthest.

**neighborhood** (NAY-ber-hood)  The area in which you live.

**pentathlon** (pen-TATH-lon)  A contest in which athletes have to finish five different events.

**professional** (pro-FESH-in-ul)  Someone who gets paid to play a sport.

**record** (REH-kerd)  The highest score in a sport.

**scholarship** (SKAH-ler-ship)  An award of money so students who are good athletes can go to college.

**track and field** (TRAK AND FEELD)  A group of contests in which athletes run, jump, and throw heavy weights.

# Index